DUST DEVIL

A miniature whirlwind whips up dust and sand into the air. Dust and sand storms are common whenever the wind blows strongly over the open desert. A storm blowing sand over 3,000 metres (9,800 ft) high can suddenly appear on the horizon and engulf everything almost without warning. The dust or sand is so thick that not even the glaring desert Sun can be seen through it.

DESERT SAND

The great, constantly shifting dunes are formed by the wind, making it almost impossible for any desert plant to take root and grow. Sandy deserts are not as common as other types – deserts covered by rocks and stones make up three-quarters of the world's deserts. These sand dunes in Namibia are among the tallest in the world, reaching heights of 370 metres (1,200 ft).

FLASH FLOOD

Rainfall can happen very suddenly in some desert regions. Sometimes the rain can last for hours, even days. The massive amounts of water cover the land, cascade over rocks and fill deep ravines. Often they create deep channels as they move, carrying tonnes of sand and rocks with them. Flash floods usually occur in the mountain regions of deserts. The water may travel many kilometres from the site of the rainfall.

GHOST TOWN

This building is in the abandoned diamond mining town of Kolmanskop in Namibia. Although the desert sand has all but swallowed up the town, buildings and items, such as machinery, cars, beds and tables, are likely to remain intact for hundreds of years. This is because the desert has a preserving effect. The lack of moisture means that wood, leather, fibre and other natural materials do not perish or rot away, and metal does not rust and crumble into dust. Thus, deserts have a long memory – the abandoned signs of human activity scar the environment for many generations unless they are removed.

DESERTS OF THE WORLD

D eserts are found across the world, but most are found between the Tropics of Cancer and Capricorn, in areas where the strong Sun and hot wind bring little rain. The Sahara and Kalahari Deserts of Africa are of this type. Deserts are also found in the shelter of mountain ranges, such as the North American deserts of the Great Basin and Mojave. They are called rainshadow deserts because as the moist winds cross the mountains, they lose their moisture in the form of rain. By the time the winds reach the plains beyond the mountain peaks, there is little or no moisture left. The desert of central Australia and the Gobi Desert of Asia exist because they are too far from the sea – the rain-carrying winds simply never reach them.

DESERT HOMES

This thatched granary, which stores food, stands in a village in the Thar Desert of India. The villagers have learned how to make the best use of any rainfall. One way is to build walls around their fields, so that the rain water will not rush over the land and erode the soil. The walls trap the water, allowing it to soak into the ground and feed the plants.

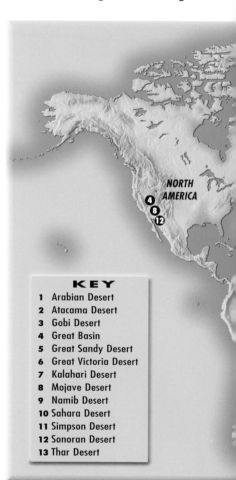

NORTH AMERICA

KEY

1 Arabian Desert
2 Atacama Desert
3 Gobi Desert
4 Great Basin
5 Great Sandy Desert
6 Great Victoria Desert
7 Kalahari Desert
8 Mojave Desert
9 Namib Desert
10 Sahara Desert
11 Simpson Desert
12 Sonoran Desert
13 Thar Desert

MONUMENT VALLEY

This spectacular desert area on the Arizona-Utah border in the USA is a rock desert which was formed by erosion over millions of years. The cliff-like rock formations, called buttes, which are hundreds of metres high, are made from sandstone. The rock is worn away by the wind and, occasionally, water. The valley floor itself is bare and flat, and is strewn with the broken fragments and fine particles of the rock slabs of fallen buttes.

THE HOSPITABLE DESERT

This map shows the desert regions of the world (shaded yellow). Most have a very hot climate, but a few that lie outside of the tropics are cool. Both arid (dry and almost without water) and semi-arid regions have low rainfall. The arid regions have an annual rainfall of less than 25 cm (10 inches), and often much less. Semi-arid regions receive between 25 and 50 cm (10-20 inches).

TROPIC OF CANCER
EQUATOR
TROPIC OF CAPRICORN

t is midday. Directly overhead the Sun burns fiercely in a cloudless sky. The glare is so strong that it makes your eyes hurt. The scorched ground stretches out all around you. In the distance the rocks shimmer from the intense heat. All is silent. Nothing moves. The desert is lifeless. Or is it? At first sight, the sun-baked land of the desert is a barren place unable to support any kind of animal or plant life whatsoever. But, in fact, most deserts are full of life – the animals are simply avoiding the hottest time of the day. Wait until the Sun is lower in the sky and the heat has lessened, and you will see the desert begin to come alive. So even though you would find the desert a difficult place to live, it is home to many animals and plants, specially adapted to the harsh conditions.

LIVING IN THE DESERT

This woman is from the Tuareg tribe, a group of people from Africa's vast Sahara Desert. They are nomads, moving from place to place looking for grazing grounds for their herds. The Tuaregs keep sheep and goats, and use camels to carry water and provide milk. Most humans cannot live easily in the desert conditions, yet desert tribes have successfully adapted to the hardships. Over many centuries they have learned how to use the land, plants and animals to survive.

WEATHER & CLIMATE

Deserts are places where no one knows for certain when it will rain next. Months and even years may pass between rainfalls. And in some desert areas, such as in the Atacama Desert of South America, it may never rain at all. This lack of rain contributes to the dryness of the deserts, which is often made worse by the hot, dry winds that blow over them. In the daytime, the ground temperature can soar to over 80°C (176°F). In these conditions, a light shower of rain from passing clouds instantly evaporates before it touches the ground, and the precious rainfall is lost. As the Sun sets, the temperature drops sharply because there are no clouds to stop the heat from escaping into the sky. As a result, it is not unusual for deserts to be frosty at night. Thus deserts have the biggest temperature ranges in any one day.

COLD DESERTS

Some deserts are among the coldest places on Earth. In extreme Arctic areas (above) it is the cold, rather than the heat and lack of moisture, that makes it difficult for life to survive. Water is locked up in snow and ice. In tundra regions, vast treeless zones of the far north where the subsoil is permanently frozen, there is a brief summer when some of the snow melts, and plants and animals can get the water they need to flourish and reproduce.

UNDER A CLOUDLESS SKY

From space, the Atacama Desert of South America can be clearly seen. This desert is sandwiched between the Andes, the mountain chain that runs down the entire west coast of the continent, and the Pacific Ocean. The Andes act as a barrier to rain-bearing clouds blown across from the west. In addition, the effect of the Humboldt Current, a cold sea current that flows along the coastal edge of South America, is to dry the sea air before it reaches the land. This desert is one of the driest regions in the world.

PACIFIC OCEAN THE ANDES

ATACAMA DESERT

DESERTS LONG AGO

These beautiful rock paintings show that the Sahara region was once a less arid place, able to support those animals that are found today on the great grassy plains of the African savanna. The drawings were made around 5,000 years ago, when the climate of North Africa was much wetter. As the climate changed and the weather became hotter, the lakes and water holes slowly began to dry out, creating the desert we know today.

THE SAHARA DESERT

The Sahara Desert in North Africa is the largest desert in the world. It covers almost a third of the African continent, and is almost the size of the United States. The great camel caravans seen on the Sahara are usually controlled by the Tuareg people, who traditionally travelled across vast areas of the desert to trade. But not all of the Sahara is sand. The sandy regions, called ergs, only make up one-fifth of the area – the rest is made up of mountains, stony plateaus and dust-filled basins.

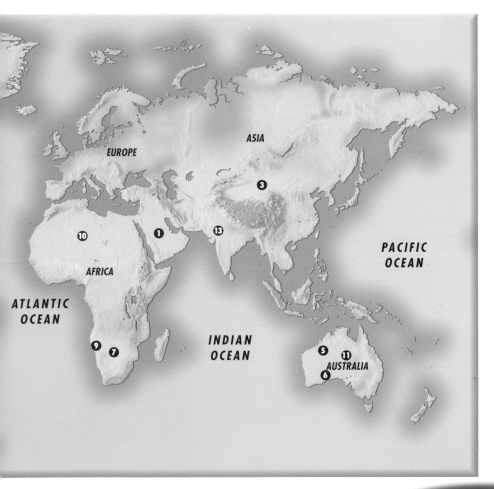

THE SIMPSON DESERT

The Simpson Desert is a region of about 145,000 sq km (56,000 sq miles) in central Australia. Here sand dunes up to 35 metres (115 ft) high and 450 metres (1,500 ft) apart run parallel across the desert. In between these sand-dune crests grows spinifex grass, which is specially adapted to the dry desert conditions. The Simpson Desert is home to some of the most unique desert animals, such as marsupial mice, but these have become threatened since the introduction of the cat to Australia.

DESERT PLANTS

Plants have evolved special ways of living in the desert. Only the shifting sand dunes are plant free, as it is impossible for the plants to establish themselves. But elsewhere, plants are able to exist, and have adapted in a variety of ways. They have to survive long periods of drought. The rain, when it comes, is unpredictable – it could be a light shower or it could fall in torrents. Many plants deal with these extremes by taking every drop of moisture they can take up into their roots and storing it in their stems, or in underground tubers (fleshy roots).

ANNUAL PLANTS

In the desert, some plants, such as this yellowtop, avoid the problem of the drought by remaining as seeds. When it rains, the seeds suddenly sprout and the plant grows very quickly, taking advantage of the moisture in the soil before it dries up. The plant flowers and then produces seeds ready for the next time it rains. After seeding, the plant dies.

Englemann's prickly pear

CACTUS FLOWERS

Cactuses produce some of the most beautiful and colourful flowers in the desert. Some cactuses have only one flower at a time, while others have many. The flowers only last for a short time – from a single night in some cases to several days in others.

Claw cactus

GIANT SAGUARO CACTUS

These giant plants of the North American deserts can reach a height of 16 metres (52 ft) and a weight of 10 tonnes. They send out a network of shallow roots up to 10 metres (33 ft) in all directions. The roots are strong and dense to both absorb as much water as possible and keep the plant upright in strong winds. These majestic cactuses take a very long time to grow – this one may be over 200 years old.

Cactuses suck up water when it rains and hoard it in their stems, using it gradually to grow during the long periods of drought. When there is another downpour, they can refill their tanks.

Leaves have been reduced to spines, to minimize water loss and to protect the plant

Ribs or pleats expand when it rains to store water in its sponge-like cells

Stem has a waxy surface to stop water loss

Roots spread out near the surface to take up rain water

TUNISIAN OASIS

Oases are natural springs fed by water that comes from a distant source, such as rain-fed mountains, maybe hundreds of kilometres away. The water flows underground through the rock until the rock comes to the surface. Desert people live by oases as the surrounding area is very fertile. There, plants and trees flourish, such as these palms, which dates grow on. In Australia, oases are called billabongs.

CREOSOTE BUSH

This bush flourishes when there is lots of space around it. It spreads its roots and absorbs the moisture that has collected a few centimetres below the surface of the soil. It collects the water so effectively that no other plants can grow within several metres of it. The waxy coating on the leaves helps to stop water escaping.

DESERT OAKS

These trees in the Simpson Desert of Australia send down long roots, called tap roots, deep in the soil in search of water. A network of roots at every level ensures that the trees capture every drop of moisture that is in the soil. Plants that grow on valley floors often use this method to absorb water. Tap roots may grow tens of metres in order to reach an underground water supply.

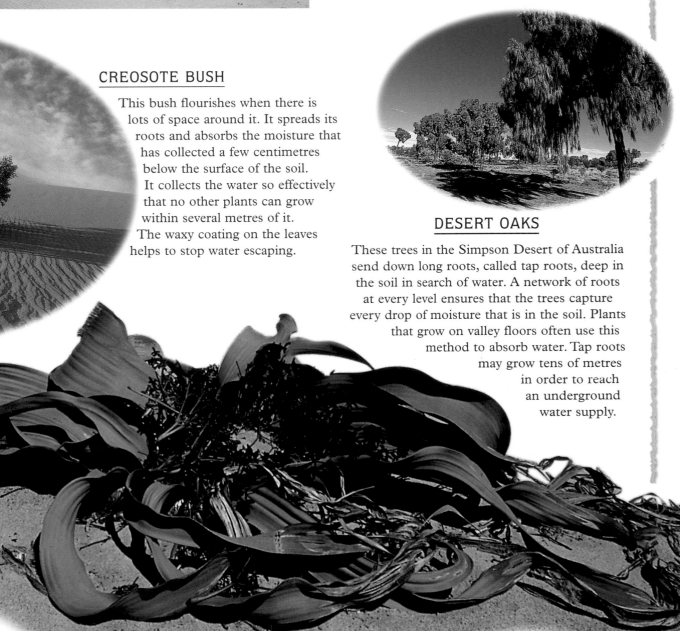

WELWITSCHIA

This unusual-looking plant grows in the Namib Desert. The Namib is situated next to the coast and at night fog often rolls in from the sea, leaving drops of moisture on the ground and on the plants. The Welwitschia has a fat, swollen root, from which grow long, strap-like leaves that can absorb water droplets. Any water that is not taken up runs off the leaves to be collected by the plant's roots.

DAYTIME CREATURES

I n the desert, the Sun beats down on the exposed land for most of the day. There are no clouds to absorb the sunlight and any vegetation gives little shade. By midday, the soil and rocks are unbearably hot to touch, so it is not surprising that desert animals seek shade during the hottest part of the day. Nothing moves unless absolutely necessary. So daytime creatures are at their most active when the Sun is not so hot – in the morning and late afternoon – when there is less danger of their bodies over-heating.

BIRD OF PREY

By staying well above the baking ground and the layer of hot air above it, the buzzard is less affected by the intense heat. Flying also creates a stream of air across its feathers, which helps to cool its body. Birds can also find high places on which to perch – perhaps a tall cactus – which are not as hot as the ground below. In addition, from their lofty vantage points, buzzards and other birds of prey can easily spot a lizard or bird that would make a good meal.

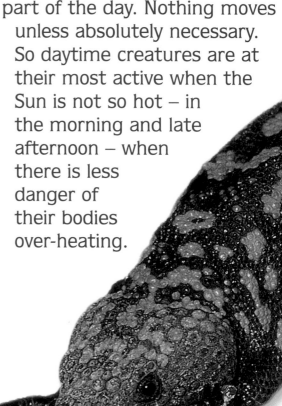

DESERT LOCUST

Locusts are large grasshoppers. They have a skeleton on the outside of the body, called an exoskeleton, which is covered in a waterproof layer of wax to prevent water loss. They get all the water they need from the plants they eat. They fly in vast swarms, sometimes in their billions, devouring crops and natural vegetation.

FERAL CAMELS

In the 19th century, one-humped camels of Arabia, called dromedaries, were brought into Australia to help people explore the desert. Now they can be found roaming ?, spending the day grazing on ?sses and scrub. The two-humped ?trian camels of the Gobi desert ? roam wild.

TIGER SWALLOWTAIL

The beautiful tiger swallowtail butterfly feeds from a flower. These insects get their moisture from nectar, the sweet-tasting liquid found at the base of many flowers. Butterflies use their long tongues to suck up the nectar, and as they move around the flower their bodies pick up pollen. When the butterfly visits a similar type of flower, some of the pollen is transferred and the flower is pollinated, and can now produce seeds.

GILA MONSTER

This American lizard begins its hunt when the Sun rises above the horizon. At first it moves about sluggishly and then, as its body warms up, it becomes more and more active as it looks for food – insects, lizard eggs, young birds and small desert mice. However, as the Sun starts to become unbearable it needs to find shade. The gila monster is the largest North American lizard, growing to 60 cm (2 ft) and its bite is poisonous – its Mexican relative is the only other poisonous lizard.

TARANTULA

This Mexican red-kneed tarantula lives in the deserts of Mexico and the southern USA. It hides in its silk-lined nest for most of the day and then emerges in the afternoon, using its long, hairy legs to catch its prey, which are mainly beetles and other insects. It uses poisoned fangs to kill its food and protect itself from attack.

WHAT A LARK!

Of all the desert creatures, birds are the ones that cope with the intense heat most easily. Their feathers are good insulators. When it is cold the feathers keep the bird warm. But feathers are also good at keeping the heat out. This makes it possible for birds to sit in the desert sun without over-heating. When birds get too hot, they reduce their temperature by fluttering their throats. This desert lark is active throughout most of the day.

NIGHT-TIME CREATURES

EASTERN SCREECH OWL

Like most owls, this bird is nocturnal. It is a bird of prey – it hunts other animals for food – and stays comfortable in its nest-hole during the day, conserving its energy. But as night falls, it leaves its home to search for the mice, insects and lizards that become active after dark. The screech owl is well adapted to hunting at night. Extremely good eyesight and very sensitive hearing enable it to locate its prey. Its feathers help it to stay warm in the cold hours of darkness.

A s darkness falls, the temperature begins to drop. Cold-blooded creatures (animals unable to make heat to warm their bodies, such as lizards) loose their warmth quickly and so must retire to their burrows when it gets too cold. However, for most desert creatures the coolness is a welcome relief from the stifling heat, and they stir from their day-time slumber as the Sun begins to set. For them the hours of darkness are the best time to be active. Small mammals, such as desert mice, move about timidly looking for seeds and bits of dead vegetation to eat. By dawn, the ground and rocks will have lost nearly all the stored heat from the previous day. This is the coldest time of the day, and many of the nocturnal animals return to their holes and crevices. Soon the daytime creatures will be on the move, often led by the birds, which are the desert's early risers.

NIGHT-TIME TRACKS

Sometimes the only evidence of night-time creatures is their tracks in the sand.

FENNEC FOX *SIDEWINDER SNAKE* *KANGAROO RAT*

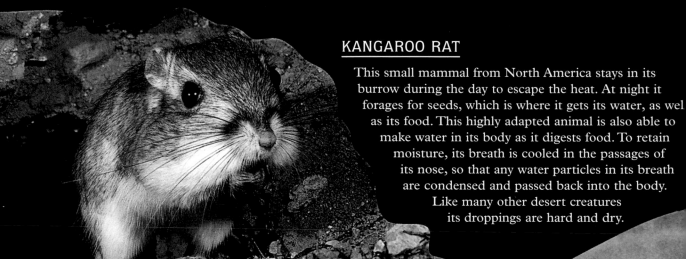

KANGAROO RAT

This small mammal from North America stays in its burrow during the day to escape the heat. At night it forages for seeds, which is where it gets its water, as wel as its food. This highly adapted animal is also able to make water in its body as it digests food. To retain moisture, its breath is cooled in the passages of its nose, so that any water particles in its breath are condensed and passed back into the body. Like many other desert creatures its droppings are hard and dry.

NIGHT-HUNTING GECKO

Although most lizards are daytime hunters, not all lizards retire to their crevices as soon as the Sun goes down – as long as the earth and rocks still retain some warmth, they are able to continue to hunt for food. This gecko is from the deserts of central Asia. It grows to 20 cm (8 inches) in length, and lives in a burrow.

HOTSON'S FIVE-TOED JERBOA

The jerboa can be found in the Sahara Desert. It has short, weak forelimbs, long hind limbs and a long tail, making it look like a small kangaroo. It ventures out of its nest as soon as night falls, in the hope that the darkness will give it some protection from fennec foxes and other enemies. As the jerboa hops about, it looks for seeds, tufts of grass and other bits and pieces of plants that make up its diet. Some of its food may have been blown into its area by the wind.

FENNEC FOX

hese hunters of the Sahara Desert have large triangular ears for picking up the sounds made by gerbils and other small animals as they camper around the desert looking for food. Fennec foxes move silently, their noses to the ground, sniffing for a scent trail that hy lead to a tasty meal. Its large eyes help it to see in the darkness of the night.

FINDING WATER

Water is essential for life – it replaces lost fluids and is vital for many body processe[s]. So how are desert creatures able to surviv[e] the hot, dry conditions that can last for months, or even years, before there is even a drop of rain? The answer is that they have all found ways of conserving water. A few of them do not even need to drink. They either get what little water they need from their food or they make it in their bodies as part of the process of turning food int[o] body fuel. Birds have the advantage of being able to [fly] to a source of water. Other animals make long journeys to find the water they need[.]

A WATER CARRIER

Sand grouse build their nests up to 40 km (25 miles) from a pool. When the eggs hatch, the males ferry water back to their chicks in their feathers. As they paddle in the pool, their breast feathers become wet, and when they are fully saturated they fly back to the nest where the chicks 'suck' the water off with their beaks.

WATER FROM PLANTS

Like some other large desert animals, the dorca[s] gazelle of Africa finds mu[ch] of the water it needs fro[m] the plants it eats. The lea[ves] contain the plants' sap, a[nd] this watery fluid is enoug[h] for the gazelle to survive.

AT THE WATER HOLE

The red kangaroo, one of the largest of the kangaroo family, is found all over Australia, including the desert regions. It gets very little water from the grasses it eats, and so the kangaroo makes a trip from its grazing grounds to a water hole every day. Red kangaroos live in herds, or mobs, of around 10 to 15 animals.

CATCHING WATER

This beetle from the Namib Desert takes advantage of the fog that often hangs over the desert at night. It climbs to the top of a sand dune and stands facing the sea with its head downwards and its body lifted up into the air. As water droplets form on its body, they roll down into the beetle's mouth.

FRUIT JUICE

The fruits of plants are a good source of water. These are the fruit of the prickly pear, which are moist and juicy. Birds, beetles and other creatures that eat these fruits have little need of drinking water.

OPEN WIDE

The road runner is a bird often seen running across the deserts of North America on its slender legs. The adult bird feeds its chicks by dropping food – a lizard or snake – into the chick's gaping mouth, and in doing so trickles water from its beak into the throat of the chick, allowing it to drink.

BODY FLUIDS

The desert jackal hunts animals for food, and the kill provides it with enough water so that it does not need to make special trips to a water hole. The water is in the form of body fluids, which it swallows as it feeds. For example, blood is a body fluid, and about half of it is made up of a substance called plasma, which is mainly water.

COOLING DOWN

The emu is a large flightless bird that lives in most parts of Australia, including the desert areas. They cope with the heat of the desert quite well, and when they need to cool themselves, they flutter their throats to lose heat.

WATER RETENTION

Some species of toad survive well in the desert dryness. They store up to half their body weight of water in their bladder. Desert toads are able to survive an extremely long

SURVIVING THE HEAT

The best way of surviving the heat is simply to avoid it. So the majority of desert animals rest in the daytime in a cool burrow or crevice in the rocks. Those that do not go underground find shade to wait out the heat, though this can be difficult in deserts where vegetation is sparse with few leaves to cast large shadows. Even the slightest movement of a leg or the head produces heat in an animal's body, so at the hottest time of the day most animals keep as still as possible. Even lizards and snakes, which need warmth in order to be active, are at the mercy of the hot conditions. Their bodies would dangerously over-heat if they stayed out in the open.

SUN SHADE

This ground squirrel is active during the daytime, taking its portable 'umbrella' with it wherever it goes. When it gets too hot, it erects its bushy tail over its head and spreads the hairs so that it casts as wide a shadow as possible. It cocks its tail to adjust the position of the shadow so that it always falls on its body.

This African lizard (below) is perfectly adapted to the harsh conditions found in desert dunes. It is called a sand swimmer from the way it appears to swim through the sand with fish-like movements of its body. The surface of the dune gets unbearably hot in the daytime, but just a few centimetres below the surface it is much cooler. The grains of sand are so smooth and dry that the lizard is able to swim through the sand to where a beetle is moving around on the surface. It then pops out to seize the beetle in its strong jaws.

WATERTIGHT SKIN

This horned viper's watertight skin allows it to retain all the water in its body.

COOL EARS

The huge ears of the North American jack rabbit act like radiators to give off heat.
A fine network of blood vessels running just under the skin cool down the rabbit's body, as air blows over its ears.

Heavy tail is an aid to 'swimming'

Small legs which it holds close to its body when 'swimming' through the sand

Fringes on its feet allow it to run on the surface of the dune

Skin does not sweat so water is conserved

Tight-fitting scales and stream-lined shape for travelling quickly through the sand

Sharp, chisel-shaped nose for pushing the sand aside as it travels forwards

Sunken ears for smooth shape

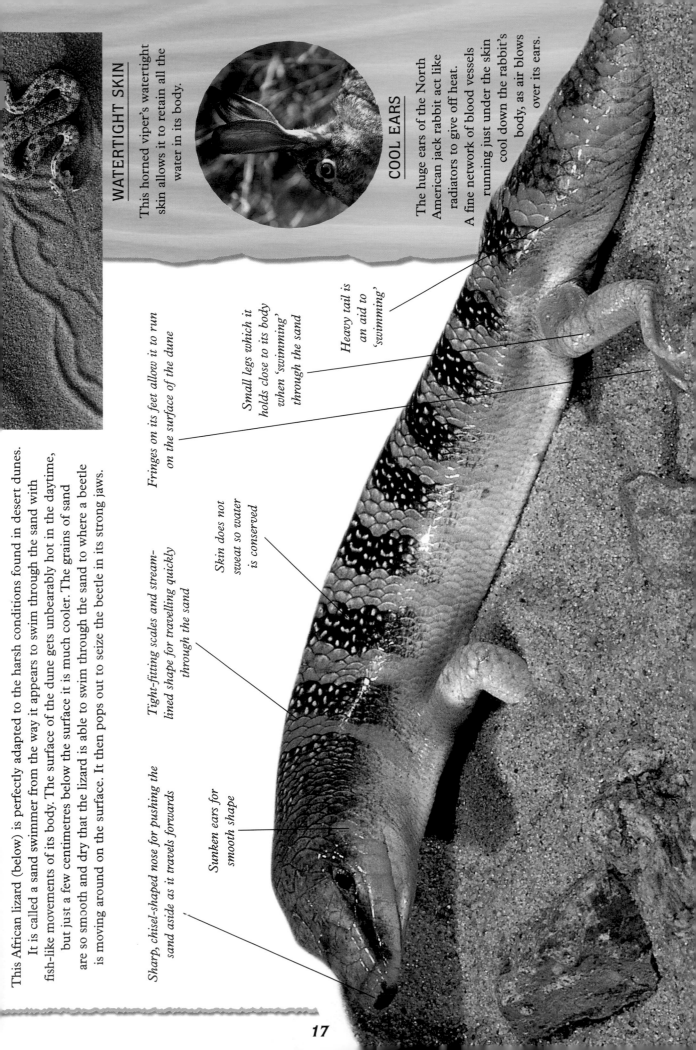

WHEN IT RAINS

FAIRY SHRIMP

Swarms of tiny fairy shrimp swim in muddy pools left by a cloudburst. They appear so fast that it is as if they had fallen with the rain. In fact, they have hatched from eggs that have been in the soil or blown on the wind since the last rain – which in some instances may be as long as 50 years ago. They are in a hurry to grow and mate before the puddles dry out and they die. By the time all the water has gone, their eggs have been laid ready for the next generation of these tiny creatures.

For most of the year, the desert looks barren and it is a wonder that animals and plants exist there at all. Often the richness of life is a surprise, and only really becomes obvious when it rains. This is the trigger that brings the parched, dry earth to life, for there are many creatures and plants that cram all the active parts of their life cycle into one short period when water is abundant. Until the downpour, they remain dormant and unseen, but afterwards they flourish, reaching maturity with incredible speed before the puddles and lakes dry up in the Sun. Then when all the water has evaporated and the land is once again dry and parched, all that is left is their shrivelled remains. But they have fulfilled their purpose – to reproduce and ensure there are future generations of life.

SPADEFOOT TOAD

The gift of water is too much to miss for the spadefoot toad, for this is the signal for the toa to emerge from the soil, where it buries itself, mate in the pools of water. Once the eggs are lai and fertilised, the toads hop away to feed. They m build up their reserves before they again burrow int the ground to wait for the next fall of rain. In the mear time, the eggs develop very fast. Within a day o two the pool is swarming with tadpole which must finish their development before the pool dries out. Only a few will mature into toads and make their home in the dese

BLOOMING DUNE

After a shower of rain the desert can become a riot of colour. On the right, evening primrose plants are flowering in the shifting sand of the Sonoran Desert in the USA.

DEVIL'S CLAW SEED POD

s weird 'growth' is a devil's claw seed pod. In the desert, seed heads and pods quickly become brown and dry, and dead looking. But as soon as re is a cloudburst, they appear to come to life, for the rainwater causes the parts to split allowing the seeds to fall to the ground and grow.

ALGAE

The dust that blows around the desert contains microscopic spores – cells that are so small that they can only be seen under a microscope. In the pools these develop into the filaments of simple plants called algae. The algae grow fast and reproduce not by mating, but by shedding more microscopic spores into the water. When the pool dries up, the algae dies. However, the spores have a tough skin and are able to withstand the hot desert conditions. They blow about the desert until the next fall of rain.

BEFORE AND AFTER

The semi-arid region of Namaqualand in South Africa is shown here before and after the rain. The picture on the left shows the dry parched landscape. The picture on the right shows the desert after the rain, when dormant seeds have suddenly burst into life.

HAWK

LIZARD

BEETLE

Large birds of prey, such as the hawk, prey on smaller animals, including lizards and rodents. These feed on the many beetles and insects which live in the desert.

FROM PREDATOR TO PREY

This desert cat has caught a sand viper, a poisonous snake. The snake was probably on the look out for its own prey, perhaps a mouse, when it was caught. Carnivores are often food for other meat eaters.

PREDATORS & PREY

For almost any animal, the desert is a dangerous place, not only because of the heat and lack of moisture, but also because many creatures are the prey of larger animals. The busiest feeding activity occurs when th heat of the day has passed – in the late afternoon and into the evening. This is whe many creatures come out of their burrows nest holes to find food. Fortunately for bot daytime and night-time feeders most deserts have large numbers of invertebrate such as spiders, ants and beetles, which ar the staple food for many birds, rodents and reptiles. In turn, these become prey for the larger meat-eating predators. In the desert, most predators have adapted themselves in clever ways to survive the conditions.

LOOKING FOR BUGS

The pointed face and spines of the desert hedgehog of North Africa are very similar to hedgehogs found in European countries. However, their ears are larger. This helps them to catch every sound in the desert. Their large ears also help them to lose heat. The desert hedgehog is always on the search for beetles and other insects on its nightly forages.

SAHARAN CHEETAH

A desert cheetah in West Africa runs down its prey. It can reach a speed of 96 km/h (60 mph), but only over a short distance, after which it will usually give up if it has not caught its prey. Top predators like cheetahs also provide food for scavengers like vultures and hyenas.

A THORNY DEVIL

This weird-looking creature from Australia gets its name from the thorn-like spikes that cover its body. Also called the moloch lizard, its method of feeding is to sit by a trail of ants and flick them up into its mouth using its tongue. It can eat several thousand ants at any one time. Since the ants are eaten one by one, the meal can take quite some time!

A DEADLY HUG

A kingsnake of North America grasps the head of a mouse while it uses its body to squeeze its prey to death. Kingsnakes are so-called because they kill and eat other snakes, including the venomous rattlesnake, one of the most feared creatures of the desert. The kingsnake is immune to the venom of other snakes, and so its victims have been known to try and beat off their attacker with their body rather than defend themselves by biting.

COMING UP FOR A MEAL

The golden mole is a dune-living predator, tunnelling through the sand and coming above ground to catch insects, like this locust.

FOOD CHAIN

FENNEC FOX

DESERT MOUSE

SEEDS

Foxes pounce on mice as they scurry around the desert looking for seeds and other plant food. Plants make their food through photosynthesis. In this way, it is the energy of the Sun that begins the desert food chain.

DEFENCE

Desert animals are in a constant battle to stay alive. Part of the battle is to escape from their predators when attacked, and so they have evolved an amazing number of ways to avoid their enemies. Some of these are very simple, such as running or hopping away at high speed when threatened. The jack rabbit, for example, can reach 70 km/h (43 mph) in a series of long springing bounds when chased by a hungry coyote. Other defences, such as camouflage, when animals simply blend into the scenery, can be equally effective.

GOING UNDERGROUND

Ground squirrels found in North America and Africa build large networks of tunnels in which they live. In North America, they make a very loud warning 'chirp' when a bird of prey soars into view before bolting for cover. If a rattlesnake comes near, they make more warning chirps and 'flag' their tails to indicate the position of the snake.

SPEED

Many animals simply flee from their attackers as fast as they can. A large predator, such as a desert fox or cat, will approach its prey by stealth, so that it can get close enough to leap. But once spotted, the prey will try to get away, with the predator giving chase. If the animal is fast enough, it will outrun its attacker and so escape.

PROTECTIVE SHELLS

Tortoises do not need speed to escape their enemies. Their defence is the armoured shell they carry around with them into which they retreat when danger threatens. They withdraw their heads completely, protecting the entrances at the front and back with their scaly skin. This allows them to feed on wild flowers and other plants at their leisure.

CAMOUFLAGE

Most desert animals have a basic colour pattern that suits their habitat, making them blend in with the background. But the chameleon has the added advantage of being able to vary its colour, thus enhancing its camouflage to escape its enemies.

BRIGHT COLOURS

In the animal world, brightly-coloured markings are a warning to other animals that a creature is nasty to eat or poisonous. The colours are designed to make them as obvious as possible. In the case of the coral snakes of North America, the bands of colour are saying, 'Keep away because I've got a poisonous bite!' As a result, most predators stay well clear of the snake and avoid attacking it.

JUST BLUFFING

Sheer bluff is the means by which this Australian frill-necked lizard repels attackers. The large photograph shows the enormous neck frill, which is the main feature of the bluff. Above is the frill fully erected. At the same time, the lizard will also stand on its hind legs and, with its mouth wide open, bob its head and lash its tail back and forth to frighten off its predator.

23

NESTS, EGGS & YOUNG

Reptiles, such as lizards and snakes, generally lay their eggs and then leave. After hatching, the young must look after themselves. Amphibians, such as frogs and toads, generally make poor parents, too. After the eggs are laid in a pool of water, the adults move on. However, other animals show some form of caring for their young. Social insects, such as ants and termites that live in colonies, have workers that tend and feed the larvae until they become adult. But it is the birds and mammals that make the most effort in raising a family. Their offspring are kept clean, fed and protected until they are old enoug to fend for themselves.

RED TAIL HAWKS

These majestic daytime hunters of the North American deserts make their ragged nests high in the prickly branches of saguaro cactuses. This helps to ensure that the eggs and chicks will not get dangerously hot in the unbearable heat of the day. The nest is built out of the reach of predators. At night, the warmth from the parents' bodies stops the chicks getting too cold as the temperature plummets.

MEERKATS

The meerkat, or suricate, of the desert country of southern Africa lives in community burrows. The young are born underground, but as they gro they begin to venture out as a group, and always the company of adult meerkats. The adults keep a constant lookout for predators, and at the slightest sign of danger they give an alarm and everyone dives for the safety of the burrow.

FENNEC FOX & HER BABIES

ammals, like this fennec fox, take excellent care of their
bies. The female fox suckles her young with milk from a
nd called a mammary gland. But first the mother builds
an underground nest called
a den, where the young
will be safe from
desert predators.
After the
babies are
born, she
feeds, cleans
and keeps
them warm.
As the babies grow,
the mother gradually
changes the diet
from milk to
solid food, bringing
them desert mice
to eat.

DESERT LOCUST

Like a lot of
other insects,
these mini-
beasts show
only a basic
form of care for
their young.
The female
uses her egg-laying
organ, or ovipositor,
to drill into the soil
before laying her eggs.
By placing them
underground she hides them
from hungry enemies.

HITCHING A RIDE

Scorpions are fearsome hunters
but they make excellent parents.
After hatching from the eggs, the young
scorpions hitch a ride on their mother's back.
There they are safe, protected by the mother's strong
pincers and deadly sting, until they are large enough
to look after themselves.

LIVING TOGETHER

Some desert animals spend their entire lives living together. In the case of insect societies, many thousands of individuals live in a colony, working together to carry out many different tasks, such as nest building, breeding and defence against enemy attack. The degree of organisation of these large communities seems incredible, as they function almost like a single creature. Because of this, they are sometimes called 'super organisms'.

Other animals that live in groups may not have the same numbers or degree of organisation, but they still depend on one another for survival.

SAFETY IN NUMBERS

A flock of ring-neck doves gather at a desert water hole to drink. There is safety in numbers for the doves, for while some of the birds are drinking, the other ones are on the lookout for enemies. This makes it very difficult for any predator to pounce on the flock by surprise.

NIGHT-TIME PARTNERS

A cactobastis moth sits on a prickly pear cactus. Instead of closing their flowers at night, some desert plants do just the opposite and open them to attract the night-time insect visitors that pollinate them. In return the insects get a rewarding meal of nectar.

GEMSBOK

Herds of this stocky animal are found in the arid region south of the Sahara Desert. The gemsbok is a type of oryx, and is well adapted to living in the desert. It feeds on dry vegetation, and can go for long periods without drinking. Its cousins once lived in large numbers in the deserts of the Sahara, and the Sinai and Arabian Peninsulas, but they were hunted to extinction. More recently, the oryx was bred in zoos and reintroduced to the wild in the 1980s.

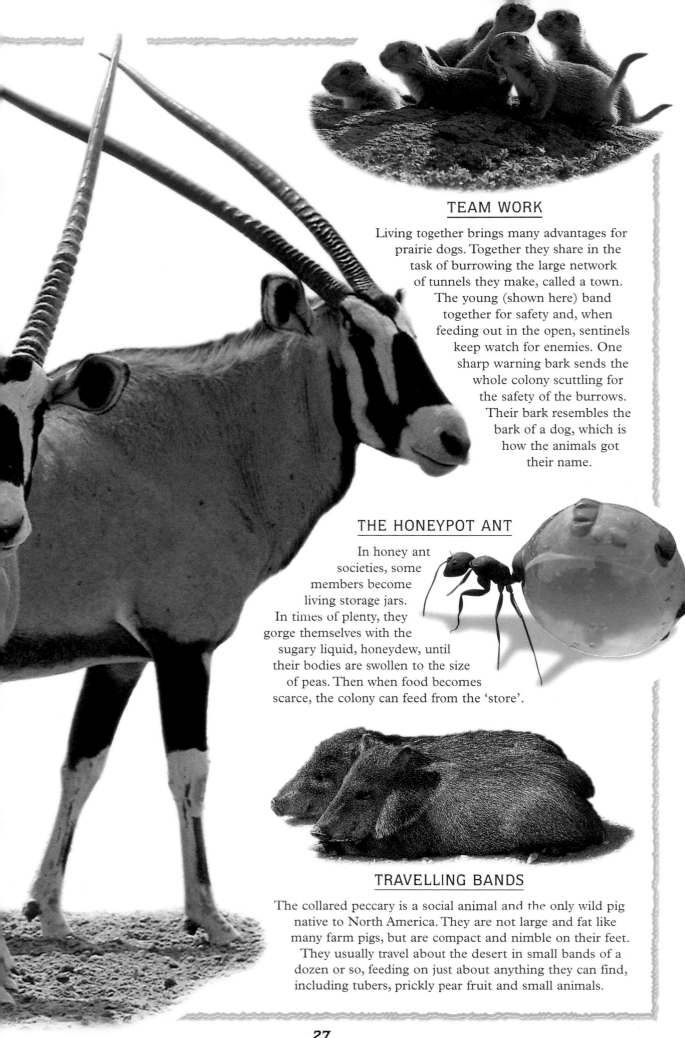

TEAM WORK

Living together brings many advantages for prairie dogs. Together they share in the task of burrowing the large network of tunnels they make, called a town. The young (shown here) band together for safety and, when feeding out in the open, sentinels keep watch for enemies. One sharp warning bark sends the whole colony scuttling for the safety of the burrows. Their bark resembles the bark of a dog, which is how the animals got their name.

THE HONEYPOT ANT

In honey ant societies, some members become living storage jars. In times of plenty, they gorge themselves with the sugary liquid, honeydew, until their bodies are swollen to the size of peas. Then when food becomes scarce, the colony can feed from the 'store'.

TRAVELLING BANDS

The collared peccary is a social animal and the only wild pig native to North America. They are not large and fat like many farm pigs, but are compact and nimble on their feet. They usually travel about the desert in small bands of a dozen or so, feeding on just about anything they can find, including tubers, prickly pear fruit and small animals.

PEOPLE OF THE DESERT

Despite the harshness of the weather conditio[ns], people who live in the desert are able to ma[ke] use of what it has to offer to support their families and make a living. For example, in North America, native American tribes, such as the Hop[i] and Navajo, learned long ago to use the plants an[d] animals of the desert for food, clothing and shelt[er]. And in Africa, the bushmen of the Kalahari Deser[t] know many secrets of the desert, including which plants have tubers that store enough water to provide a drink. Without such special knowledge, people would not survive long in the harsh desert conditions.

LIVING UNDERGROUND

The Australian town of Coober Pedy is on the edge of the virtually waterless Great Victoria Desert. Most of the world's opal gemstones are mined here. Its name means 'white man's hole', which refers to the practice of early miners who built their homes underground to escape the high temperatures.

PORTABLE HOMES

The nomads of the Gobi Desert of Central Asia move from one are[a to] another in order to find enoug[h] grass for their large flocks of animals to feed on. Their hom[es,] called yurts, can be put up, taken down and transpor[ted] very easily. The Gobi Desert is one of the largest deserts in th[e] world, about 1,600 km (1,000 miles) long and 1,000 km (625 miles) wide.

AUSTRALIAN ABORIGINES

The Aborigines of the Australian desert are able to supply all their needs from the land. For example, they know which different areas, whether rocky hills or sand dunes, provide the particular species of plants they require or animals to hunt. They know where the water holes are, and they reach the water in dry creek beds by digging away the sand until water seeps into the hole.

FRUITS OF THE DESERT

People living close to oases are able to irrigate the land and produce crops. Often palm trees are grown for their harvest of dates, which may be spread out on the ground to dry in the Sun.

PEOPLE OF THE SAHARA

Even the great dune deserts of the Sahara are inhabited by the Tuareg, a nomadic people who lead caravans of camels with goods to trade. They carry cloth, dates, precious metals and other goods to sell or exchange at ancient trading cities for the things they need, such as salt. The nomads wear long flowing cloaks and cover their faces to protect them from the Sun.

CAL ATERIALS

Moroccan sket-maker displays his wares. The people of desert regions have learnt to live in harmony with their environment, taking only what they need in order to survive. By using local resources wisely for producing items for sale or building materials, they put le demand on the desert.

REFORESTATION

Reforestation projects
are becoming
necessary in the
southern Sahara.
Whole villages
are becoming
involved in
such projects,
as the trees
they plant hold the
soil together and
prevent erosion from the
wind and rain. Areas that
have been cleared of trees
and shrubs are replanted
before they become part
of the advancing desert.

SALT MINES

Walvis Bay is on the
coastal margin of
the Namib Desert.
Here the sea water
slowly evaporates in
the hot Sun, leaving
behind a layer of sea salt.
Saltpans are similar, only
they form in desert basins
and rely on the evaporation
of rainwater for the surface
cover of mineral salts. Salt is a valuable item,
and in some cases the deposits are intensively
mined, with disruption to the desert
environment caused by the extraction itself
and the transport used to take the salt away.

PROTECTING THE DESERTS

The deserts are fragile places which can easily be spoilt. For example, some of the world's greatest oilfields are found in desert areas. Although oil brings much-needed resources to the countries that extracts it, the building of wells, storage tanks, oil pipelines and roads inevitably have a harmful impact on the environment. Attempts to make the desert bloom, through irrigation schemes, have also had an adverse effect in many deserts. Desert water contains high levels of mineral salts, and these build up in the soil until no plants can grow. If the animals and plants of the desert are to survive, such as the endangered Gila monster lizard of North America, they must be protected from the thoughtless actions of people.

OIL WELLS

An oil well in Kuwait burns out of control after it was set alight by Iraqi forces. Pollution ruined large areas of desert during the Gulf War in early 1991.

OVER-GRAZING

The number of people living permanently along the desert margin has increased in recent years. The people farm the land, cutting down trees for fuel and keeping herds of grazing animals, such as goats. This has put great pressure on the already sparse vegetation, which is not given enough time to recover properly. As a result the edge of the desert slowly advances, reducing the area for farming.

CITIES IN THE DESERT

Many cities have sprung up in desert regions, such as Las Vegas in the Nevada Desert in the USA, famous for its luxury hotels and casinos. The inhabitants of desert cities live and work in air-conditioned buildings. The huge supply of water a city demands cannot usually be met locally. So it must be piped in from rivers or reservoirs perhaps hundreds of kilometres away. A good road network encourages more and more people to visit the desert, diminishing the areas that are left unspoilt.

THE SPREADING DESERT

Along the margins of many deserts are zones of semi-desert. These zones are not true desert, but regions where the rainfall is enough for crops to grow. As more people settle in these areas to farm the land, these areas are turning into desert by poor farming techniques. The map shows the risk of desertification in northwest Africa. The problem was made worse by a severe drought from 1969 to 1973. This led to the first ever United Nations conference on desertification in 1977.

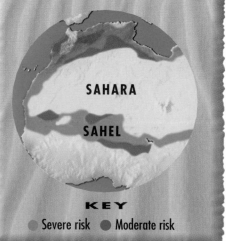

SAHARA

SAHEL

KEY
● Severe risk   ● Moderate risk

GLOSSARY

Cloudburst An extreme form of rainfall that only lasts a few minutes but often creates floods.

Desertification Areas where the land has turned to desert after the soil has been overused by people.

Exoskeleton A hard covering on the outside of an animal's body, which protects its soft inside.

Invertebrate An animal that does not have a backbone, such as an ant.

Ovipositor A tubular-shaped organ which an insect or fish deposits its eggs with.

Nomads People who constantly move from one place to another to find food for themselves and their animals.

Saltpan A flat area in the desert where water has evaporated to leave behind salt and other minerals.

Savanna A tropical grassland with a scattering of shrubs and trees.

Reforestation The planting of trees and seeds to regrow forest that has been burnt, or cut down.

Tubers The fleshy, underground roots of a plant which are used to store water and food.

ACKNOWLEDGMEN

We would like to thank: Ben Hubbard. Artwork by Pe

Copyright © 2009 *ticktock* Entertainmen

First published in Great Britain by *ticktock* Media Ltd, The Old Sa

Tunbridge Wells, Kent TN1 2DP, Great

All rights reserved. No part of this publication may be reproduced, stored in a retrieva
electronic, mechanical, photocopying, recording or otherwise, without prior

A CIP catalogue record for this book is available from

ISBN 978 1 84898 001 3 (paperba

ISBN 978 1 84898 046 4 (hardba

Picture research by Image Select. Printed

Picture Credits: t=top, b=bottom, c=centre, l=left, r=right, OFC=outside front cover, OBC=outside back cover, IFC=inside front cover

Auscape; 8tl, 21c, 28bl. B & C Alexander Photography; 4tl. BBC Natural History Unit; 22cl. Bruce Colman Limited; 12bl, 20bl, 24tl. FLPA; 19bc, 29tl. NHPA; 15tl, 18b, 21br, 25tr, 24/25t, 26tl, 26bl. Oxford Scientific Films; IFC, 21, 2tc, 2b, 2/3c, 4br, 4/5t, 4/5c, 5cr, 6tl, 8bc, 8lb, 8lc, 8/9c, 9b, 10tl, 10bl, 10/11bc, 11c, 13tl, 14l, 14/15c, 15b, 15c, 17tl, 17r, 18tl, 18/19t, 20/21b, 22bl, 22/23t, 22/23b & OBCbl, 23tr, 27cr, 31tr. Planet Earth; 5br, 6bl, 7br, 7tl, 9rc, 9tl, 10/11t & 32, 11br, 11tr, 12tl, 13b, 13tr, 14b, 14t, 16br, 16tl, 16tr, 17bl, 19cl, 19c, 19r, 20tl, 20/21t, 22tl, 24/25r, 26/27c, 27br, 27tr, 28br, 30bl, 31c. SATC, Australian Tourist Commission; 28tl. Shutterstock; OFC Spectrum Colour Library; 28c, 30/31cb. Still Pictures; 3br, 24bl, 29r, 30c, 30tl. Telegraph Colour Library; 7tr, OBCbr.

Every effort has been made to trace the copyright holders and we apologise in advance for any unintentional omissions. We would be pleased to insert the appropriate acknowledgement in any subsequent edition of this publication.

100

things you should know about

VIKINGS

Fiona Macdonald

Consultant: Jeremy Smith

Miles Kelly

PUBLISHING

First published in 2005 by
Miles Kelly Publishing Ltd
Bardfield Centre, Great Bardfield, Essex, CM7 4SL

Copyright © Miles Kelly Publishing Ltd 2005

2 4 6 8 10 9 7 5 3 1

Publishing Director: Anne Marshall
Editor: Belinda Gallagher
Designer: Louisa Leitao
Indexer: Jane Parker

ISBN 1-84236-581-9

Printed in China

British Library Cataloguing-in-Publication Data
A catalogue record for this book is available from the
British Library

ACKNOWLEDGEMENTS
The publishers would like to thank the following artists who have
contributed to this book:

Peter Dennis   Alessandro Menchi
Mike Foster   Peter Sarson
Richard Hook   Mike Saunders
Kevin Maddison   Mike White
Janos Marffy   Rudi Vizi

Cartoons by Mark Davis at Mackerel

www.mileskelly.net
info@mileskelly.net

100

things you should know about

VIKINGS

Contents

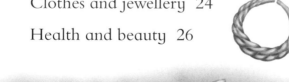

Who were the Vikings?

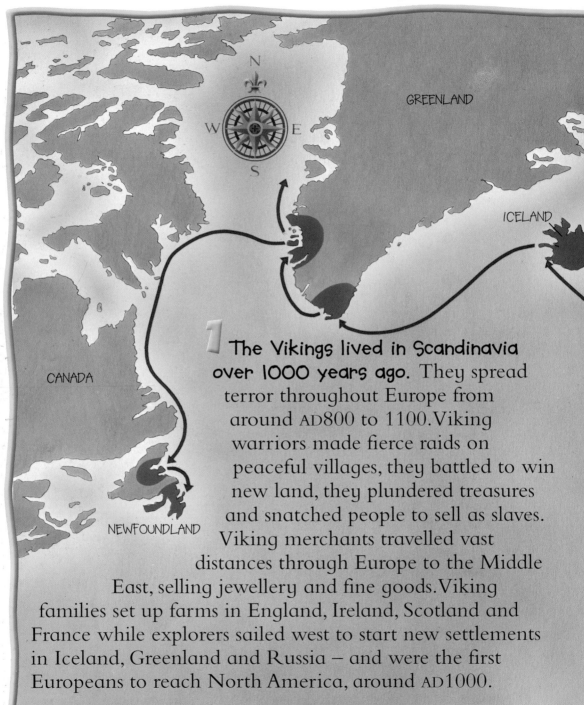

GREENLAND

ICELAND

CANADA

NEWFOUNDLAND

1 **The Vikings lived in Scandinavia over 1000 years ago.** They spread terror throughout Europe from around AD800 to 1100. Viking warriors made fierce raids on peaceful villages, they battled to win new land, they plundered treasures and snatched people to sell as slaves. Viking merchants travelled vast distances through Europe to the Middle East, selling jewellery and fine goods. Viking families set up farms in England, Ireland, Scotland and France while explorers sailed west to start new settlements in Iceland, Greenland and Russia – and were the first Europeans to reach North America, around AD1000.

▼ This map shows Viking settlements, homeland and routes of travel. The Vikings' name meant 'pirates', 'port-attackers', or 'people of the bays' – historians do not know for sure. Whichever meaning is true, it tells us that Vikings spent their lives close to the sea. They were some of the world's best, bravest sailors.

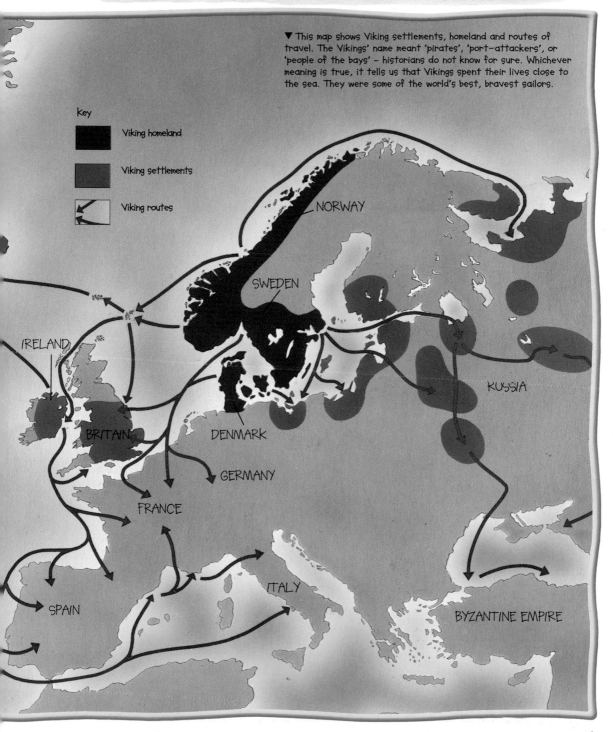

Key

Viking homeland

Viking settlements

Viking routes

NORWAY

SWEDEN

IRELAND

BRITAIN

DENMARK

GERMANY

FRANCE

RUSSIA

ITALY

SPAIN

BYZANTINE EMPIRE

Kings and people

2 **Viking society had three classes.** At the top were nobles (kings or chiefs). They were rich, owned land and had many servants. Freemen, the middle group, included farmers, traders, and craftworkers and their wives. Slaves were the lowest group. They worked hard for nobles and freemen and could not leave their owner.

Viking slave

Viking farmer

Viking noble warrior

▲ Slaves, farmers and warriors all worked hard to make Viking lands rich and powerful.

◀ Famous for his cruelty, Erik Bloodaxe was the last Viking to rule the kingdom of Northumbria, in north-east England.

3 **Viking warlords turned into kings.** During early Viking times, local chiefs controlled large areas of land. They also had armies of freemen. Over the centuries, some nobles became richer and more powerful than the rest by raiding and conquering foreign lands. By AD1050, just one noble controlled each Viking country, and called himself king.

4 **King Erik Bloodaxe killed his brothers.** When a Viking king died, each of his sons had an equal right to inherit the throne. Members of Viking royal families often had to fight among themselves for the right to rule. In AD930, King Erik of Norway killed his brothers so that he could rule alone.

5 King Harald Bluetooth left a magnificent memorial.

King Harald ruled Denmark from around AD935 to 985. He was one of the first Viking kings to become a Christian. He built a church at Jelling, the ancient Danish royal burial site, and had his parents' bodies dug up and re-buried inside. He also paid for a splendid pyramid-shaped, monument to be built next to the church, in memory of them. This 'Jelling Stone' was decorated with carvings in Viking and Christian designs.

▶ The Jelling stone (far right of picture) has carvings of a snake and a lion-like monster, fighting together. They symbolize the forces of good and evil.

6 King Cnut ruled a European empire – but not the waves!

King Cnut was one of the mightiest Viking kings. By 1028 he ruled England, Denmark and Norway. However he did not want to appear too proud. So, one day, he staged a strange event on an English beach and commanded the waves to obey him! When they did not he said, 'This proves that I am weak. Only God can control the sea.'

I DON'T BELIEVE IT!

Many Viking rulers had strange or violent names, such as Svein Forkbeard, Einar Falsemouth, Magnus Barelegs, Thorfinn Skullsplitter and Sigurd the Stout.

Sailors and raiders

7 **Vikings sailed in dragon ships.** There were different kinds of ships. Cargo ships were slow and heavy, with wide, deep hulls to carry loads. Ferry and river boats were small and sturdy, with lots of room for passengers. The most splendid ships were *drakkar* (dragon ships), designed for war. They were long, slender and speedy, with beautifully carved stern and prow. Their shallow keels helped them sail quickly onto beaches to make raids.

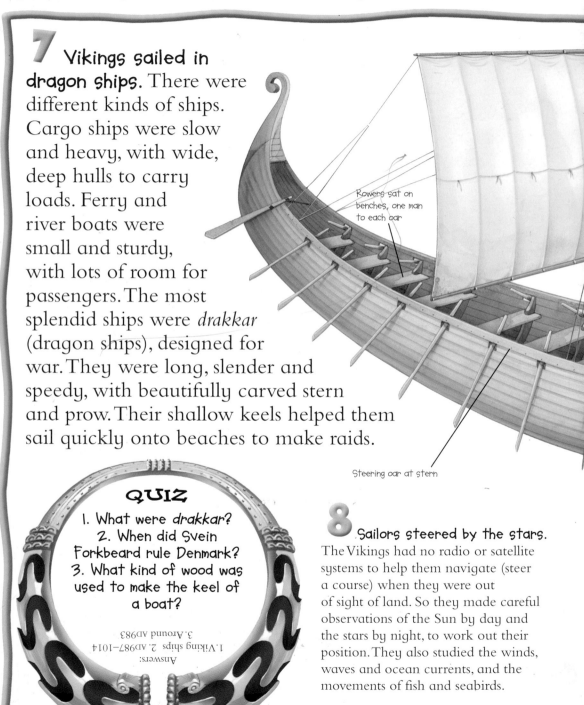

Rowers sat on benches, one man to each oar

Steering oar at stern

QUIZ

1. What were *drakkar*?
2. When did Svein Forkbeard rule Denmark?
3. What kind of wood was used to make the keel of a boat?

Answers:
1. Viking ships 2. AD987–1014
3. Around AD983

8 **Sailors steered by the stars.** The Vikings had no radio or satellite systems to help them navigate (steer a course) when they were out of sight of land. So they made careful observations of the Sun by day and the stars by night, to work out their position. They also studied the winds, waves and ocean currents, and the movements of fish and seabirds.

9 **Shipbuilders searched for tall trees.** They used oak timbers to make the keel (backbone) of each vessel. The biggest keels came from trees at least 40 metres high. Builders added long overlapping planks of oak, ash or birch, to make the hull. For masts, they used the trunks of very tall, very straight, trees, such as pine.

Square sail made of linen or wool

Carved, wooden prow

▼ A Viking dragon ship. Its long, sleek hull is made of overlapping planks of wood, held together with iron nails. Its tall mast is made from a single pine tree.

10 **Pirates demanded gold to go away.** Viking pirates such as King Svein Forkbeard of Denmark (ruled AD985–1014) demanded money with menaces! He led Viking warships to England and promised to attack if he was not paid to sail away. Svein's tactics worked. Each time he returned, the English handed over 'Dane-geld' (gold for the Danes) – again and again – and again!

Strong wooden keel (helped steer a swift, straight course through the waves)

11 **Raiders carried off treasure and slaves.** Viking nobles recruited gangs of loyal warriors to go on raiding expeditions. They sailed away from Viking homelands to attack villages or defenceless monasteries. Their aim was to grab valuable treasure and healthy young men and women to sell as slaves.

▼ Families living in seaside villages lived in constant fear of a Viking pirate raid.

Warriors and weapons

12 Vikings valued glory more than long life. They believed that a dead warrior's fame lived on after him, and made sure that his name would never die. Myths and legends also told how warriors who died in battle would go to Valhalla, where they feasted with the gods.

13 Berserkirs were mad for battle. Berserkirs ('bear-shirts') were warriors who dressed in animal skins and worked themselves into a trance before battle. They charged at the enemy, howling and growling like wolves and chewing at their shields. In this state, they were wild and fearless and dangerous to anyone who got in their way. This is where the word 'beserk' comes from.

▲ Berserkir warriors rushed madly into battle, wearing animal skins over their chain mail armour.

14 Lords led followers
into war. There were no national
armies in Viking times. Each king
or lord led his followers into battle
against a shared enemy. A lord's
followers fought to win praise, plus
rich rewards, such as arm rings of
silver or a share of captured loot.

A round shield, made of wood
covered with leather; a metal
'boss' (centre panel) protected
the warrior's hand

15 Warriors gave names to their
swords. A good sword was a Viking
warrior's most treasured possession. He
often asked to be buried with it and gave
it a name such as 'Sharp Biter'. Viking
swords were double-edged, with strong,
flexible blades made by hammering layers
of iron together. Their hilts (handles) were
decorated with silver and gold patterns.

Long sword

Knife

16 Viking soldiers lived in camps and
forts. Wars and raids took warriors far from
home. Soldiers in places such as England built
camps of wooden huts, surrounded by an
earth bank topped by a wooden wall.

Decorated iron helmet,
with a protective metal
mask around the eyes

Long, sharp spear

I DON'T
BELIEVE IT!

Viking women went to war
but they did not fight!
Instead, they nursed wounded
warriors and cooked meals
for hungry soldiers.

▲ Each Viking soldier had to provide
his own weapons and armour. Poor
soldiers wore leather caps and tunics,
and carried knives and spears. Wealthy
Vikings could afford metal helmets and
tunics, and fine, sharp swords.

Traders, explorers, settlers

17 **Viking traders rode on camels and carried their ships!** The Vikings were brave adventurers, keen to seek new land, slaves and treasures. Some traders travelled through Russia to Constantinople (now Istanbul in Turkey), and Jerusalem (in Israel). Each journey took several years. In Russia, they carried their ships over ground between rivers. In the desert near Jerusalem, they rode on camels, like local traders.

▼ Vikings made long overland journeys in winter. The frozen ground was easier to walk across — especially when carrying heavy loads.

◄ Viking merchants carried scales and weights with them on their travels.

18 **Traders carried scales and silver.** Vikings traded with many different peoples. Some used coins for trading, others preferred to barter (swap). There were no banks in Viking times and traders could not be sure of having the right money for every business deal. So they bought and sold using pieces of silver, which they weighed out on delicate, portable scales.

19 **Traders came home with lots of shopping!** Viking merchants purchased goods, as well as selling them. They went to Britain to buy wheat and woollen cloth, and to France for wine and pottery. They bought glass in Germany, jewellery in Russia, and spices from the Middle East.

20 Vikings settled from Scotland in the north of Europe to Sicily in the south. Everywhere they went, Vikings founded new villages and towns. Sometimes they fought for land from local peoples, sometimes, they lived peacefully alongside them.

21 Settlers were tricked into moving to Greenland. Erik the Red first reached the island of Greenland around AD983. It was bleak and icy, with little pasture, and almost no land suitable for grain. But Erik wanted families to join his new settlement. So he called it 'Greenland'. In AD986, Viking settlers sailed to join him. By the time they discovered what Greenland was really like, it was too late to turn back.

22 Vikings sailed to America – by mistake! In AD986, Bjarni Herjolfsson was blown off course in a storm. He saw land, but did not stop to explore. A few years later, Greenland settler Lief Eriksson decided to look for the land Bjarni had seen. He landed in places he called Hellulland, Markland and Vinland. Today, we know that these are places on the east coast of North America.

▶ The Vikings settled on Greenland's coastline as the inland areas were covered in ice. These settlements died out between 1480 and 1500 when the climate became even colder.

The Vikings at home

23 In the 700s and 800s, the Vikings were some of the best craftworkers in Europe. They lived in a harsh environment, with cold, long, dark winters. Buildings were needed to shelter livestock, as well as people. In towns, pigs, goats and horses were kept in sheds, but in parts of the countryside, farmers built longhouses, with rooms for the family at one end and for animals at the other.

24 Vikings built houses out of grass. In many lands where the Vikings settled, such as the Orkney Islands or Iceland, there were hardly any trees. So Viking families built homes out of slabs of turf (earth with grass growing in it), arranged on a low foundation of stone. If they could afford it, they lined the rooms with planks of wood imported from Scandinavia. Otherwise, they collected pieces of driftwood, washed up on shore.

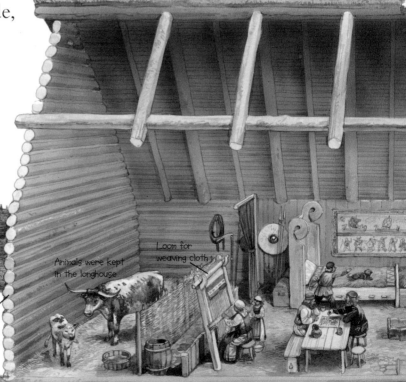

Animals were kept in the longhouse

Loom for weaving cloth

Walls made of logs

▶ Longhouses were usually built on sloping ground so that waste from the animals ran downhill, away from human living rooms.

25 Viking homes could be unhealthy. Viking houses did not have windows – they would have let in too much cold. So homes were often damp, and full of smoke from the fire burning on the hearth. As a result, Viking people suffered from chest diseases. Some may also have been killed by a poisonous gas (called carbon monoxide) that is produced when a fire uses up all the oxygen in a room.

I DON'T BELIEVE IT!

Vikings liked living in longhouses, because heat from the animals provided a kind of central heating, keeping everyone warm.

Turf (earth with growing grass) roof

Wooden rafters

Meat was smoked to preserve it

26 Homeowners sat in the high seat. Most Viking families had little furniture. Only the rich could afford beds, or tables with fixed legs. Most homes were simply furnished with trestle tables, wooden storage chests and wooden benches. The centre of one bench was marked off by two carved wooden pillars, and reserved as the 'high seat' (place of honour) for the house owner. Important guests sat facing him or her, on the bench opposite.

Outside lavatory

Farmers, fishers and hunters

27 **Viking farmers prized pasture more than ploughed fields.** In northern lands, the soil was too thin and stony for crops such as wheat and barley to grow well. Farmers relied on sheep and cattle to provide meat and milk. These animals needed fresh grass to eat so Viking farmers valued pasture land, where grass flourished, more than stony fields.

28 **Flax and hay were the most important crops.** They were needed to make clothes and feed cattle. Outer garments were made of wool, and could be very itchy, so women wove smoother, finer cloth to wear next to the skin. They used the stalks of a plant called flax, which farmers planted in damp ground. Farm animals needed hay (dried grass) to eat in winter, when pastures were covered by snow. Viking farmers grew grass in well-manured meadows, then cut it, dried it and stored it for winter.

Fish drying in the wind

Rack for drying grass to make hay

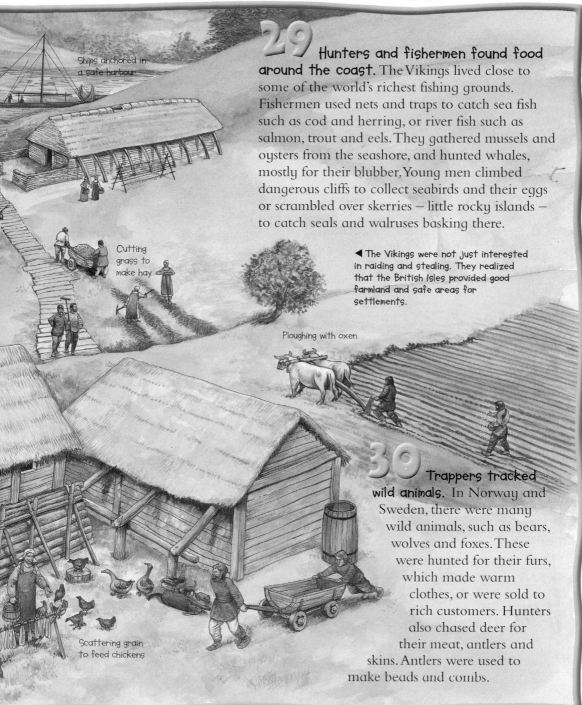

29 **Hunters and fishermen found food around the coast.** The Vikings lived close to some of the world's richest fishing grounds. Fishermen used nets and traps to catch sea fish such as cod and herring, or river fish such as salmon, trout and eels. They gathered mussels and oysters from the seashore, and hunted whales, mostly for their blubber. Young men climbed dangerous cliffs to collect seabirds and their eggs or scrambled over skerries – little rocky islands – to catch seals and walruses basking there.

◄ The Vikings were not just interested in raiding and stealing. They realized that the British Isles provided good farmland and safe areas for settlements.

Ships anchored in a safe harbour

Cutting grass to make hay

Ploughing with oxen

30 **Trappers tracked wild animals.** In Norway and Sweden, there were many wild animals, such as bears, wolves and foxes. These were hunted for their furs, which made warm clothes, or were sold to rich customers. Hunters also chased deer for their meat, antlers and skins. Antlers were used to make beads and combs.

Scattering grain to feed chickens

Food and famine

31 **Vikings ate two meals a day.** First thing in the morning was the 'day meal' of barley bread or oatcakes, butter or cheese. The main meal – 'night meal' – was eaten in the early evening. It included meat or fish, plus wild berries in summer. Meals were served on wooden plates or soapstone bowls and eaten with metal knives and wood or horn spoons.

▼ Objects made from cattle horn were light but very strong – ideal for Viking traders or raiders to carry on their journeys.

Patterned silver cup used by the rich

Pottery beaker used by the poor

Drinking horn used by warriors

QUIZ

1. What did Viking warriors drink from?
2. How did the Vikings boil water? 3. What is offal?
4. How long would a feast last for?

Answers:
1. From cow horns 2. On red-hot stones 3. The heart, liver and lungs of animals 4. A week or more

32 **Warriors drunk from hollow horns.** Favourite Viking drinks were milk, whey (the liquid left over from cheese-making), ale (brewed from malted barley), and mead (honey wine). Rich people drank from glass or silver cups, but ordinary people had wooden or pottery beakers. On special occasions feasts were held, and Viking warriors drank from curved cattle horns.

33 **Red-hot stones boiled water for cooking.** Few Viking homes had ovens. So women and their servants boiled meat in iron cauldrons, or in water-filled pits heated by stones that were made red-hot in a fire. This was a very efficient way of cooking.

Cabbage

Beans

Garlic

Peas

Onion

▲ Viking vegetables included peas, beans, cabbages, onions – and garlic.

34 **The Vikings loved blood sausages.** Cooks made sausages by pouring fresh animal blood and offal (heart, liver and lungs) into cleaned sheep's intestines, then boiling them. Sometimes they added garlic, cumin seeds or juniper berries as flavouring. Vikings preferred these to vegetables such as cabbages, peas and beans.

▼ Viking women and slaves cooked huge meals over open fires, and served them to feasting warriors.

35 **Feasts went on for a week or more.** After winning a great victory, Vikings liked to celebrate. Kings and lords held feasts to reward their warriors, and families feasted at weddings. Guests dressed in their best clothes and hosts provided much food and drink. Everyone stayed in the feast hall until the food ran out, or they grew tired.

Women and children

36 **Viking women were independent.**
They made important household
decisions, cooked, made clothes,
raised children, organized slaves and
managed farms and workshops
while their husbands were away.

▲ Women spun sheep's wool and wove it
into warm cloth on tall, upright looms.

MAKE A VIKING PENDANT

You will need:
String or cord 40 centimetres
long Modelling clay
White, yellow and brown
paint Paintbrush Gold or
or silver paint
1. Shape some animal fangs
from modelling clay, about
4 centimetres long.
2. Make a hole through the widest
end of each fang. Leave to
harden.
3. Paint the fangs with white,
brown or yellow paint. When
dry, decorate with gold and
silver paint.
4. Thread string through the fangs
and wear around your neck like
a Viking.

37 **Only widows could wed who
they wanted to.** If a Viking man
wanted to marry, he had to ask the
young woman's father for
permission and pay him a bride
price. If the father accepted this, the
marriage went ahead, even if the
woman did not agree. Widows had
more freedom. They did not need
anyone's permission to marry
again. Viking laws also gave all
women the right to ask for
a divorce if their husbands
treated them badly.

38
Old women won respect for wise advice. Many Viking women died young in childbirth or from infectious diseases. So older people, aged 50 or more, were a small minority in Viking society. While they were still fit, they were respected for their knowledge and experience. But if they grew sick or frail, their families saw them as a burden.

39
Viking fathers chose which children survived. Parents relied on children to care for them in old age so they wanted strong offspring. The father examined each baby after it was born. If it seemed healthy, he sprinkled it with water and named it to show it was part of his family. If the child looked sickly he told slaves to leave it outside to die.

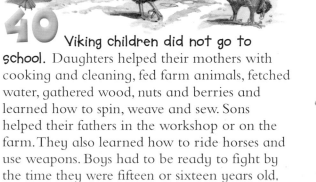

◄ Feeding chickens and collecting eggs was work for Viking girls. They learned how to grow vegetables – and cook them – by helping their mothers.

40
Viking children did not go to school. Daughters helped their mothers with cooking and cleaning, fed farm animals, fetched water, gathered wood, nuts and berries and learned how to spin, weave and sew. Sons helped their fathers in the workshop or on the farm. They also learned how to ride horses and use weapons. Boys had to be ready to fight by the time they were fifteen or sixteen years old.

▲ Viking boys practised fighting with wooden swords and small, lightweight shields.

23

Clothes and jewellery

41 **Vikings wore lots of layers to keep out the cold.** Women wore a long dress of linen or wool with a woollen over-dress. Men wore wool tunics over linen undershirts and woollen trousers. Both men and women wore gloves, cloaks, socks, and leather boots or shoes. Men added fur or sheepskin caps while women wore headscarves and shawls.

▶ Viking men and women liked bright colours and patterns. They often decorated their clothes with strips of woven braid.

42 **Furs, fleeces and feathers also helped Vikings keep warm.** Vikings lined or trimmed their woollen cloaks with fur, or padded them, like quilts, with layers of goose-down. Some farmers used sheepskins to make cloaks that were hard-wearing, as well as very warm.

43 **Brooches held Viking clothes in place.** There were several different styles. Men wore big round brooches, pinned on their right shoulders, to hold their cloaks in place. Women wore pairs of brooches — one on each shoulder — to fasten the straps of their over-dresses. They might also wear another brooch at their throat, to fasten their cloak, plus a brooch with little hooks or chains, to carry their household keys.

▶ This beautiful brooch, decorated with real gold wire, was once worn by a very rich Viking nobleman.

44 **Rings showed Vikings' wealth – and bravery.** Viking men, as well as women, liked to wear lots of jewellery. They thought it made them look good, but it also displayed their wealth, and sometimes, their achievements. Arm- and neck-rings, in particular, were often given to warriors as rewards for fighting bravely in battle.

▼ Viking craftworkers used designs from many different lands to create beautiful jewellery.

Arm–ring of twisted gold

Russian–style necklace of silver and rock crystal

Silver brooch with long pin – a typical British style

Small gold ring

45 **Favourite Viking clothing colours were red and green.** Archaeologists have found the remains of brightly-coloured cloth at Viking sites. They have also found fragments of patterned braid, silk ribbon, and gold and silver thread. All were used to decorate Viking clothes.

I DON'T BELIEVE IT!
The Vikings imported boatloads of broken glass from Germany, to melt and recycle into beautiful glass beads.

Health and beauty

46 **The English complained that Vikings were too clean!** They said that the Vikings combed their hair too often, changed their clothes frequently and bathed once a week. Vikings bathed by pouring water over red-hot stones to create clouds of steam. They sat in the steam to sweat, then whipped their skin with birch twigs to help loosen the dirt. Then they jumped into a pool of cold water to rinse off.

▲ Vikings 'bathed' in clouds of steam. Similar steam baths, called saunas, are still popular in Scandinavia today.

47 **Some Vikings took their swords to the lavatory.** Most Viking homes had an outside lavatory, consisting of a bucket or a hole in the ground with a wooden seat on top. The lavatory walls were often made of wickerwork – panels of woven twigs. But Viking warriors in enemy lands made different arrangements. They went outside in groups of four, carrying swords to protect one another.

▲ Viking lavatories may have looked like this. Vikings used dried moss, grass or leaves as toilet paper.

48 Vikings used onions to diagnose illness. If a warrior was injured in the stomach during a battle, his comrades cooked a dish of porridge strongly flavoured with onion and gave it to him to eat. They waited, then sniffed the wound. If they could smell onions, they left the man to die. They knew that the injury had cut open the stomach, and the man would die of infection.

I DON'T BELIEVE IT!

Viking men wore make-up! They particularly liked eyeliner – probably made from soot, or crushed berries. They thought it made them look more handsome.

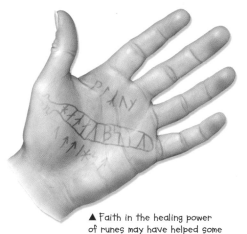

▲ Faith in the healing power of runes may have helped some Viking people feel better.

49 For painkilling power, the Vikings relied on runes. The Vikings made medicines from herbs and other plants, but they also believed that runes – their way of writing – had magic healing powers. They carved runic spells and charms on pieces of bone and left them under the heads of sleeping sick people. Runes were written on women's palms during childbirth to protect from pain.

50 Hair-care was very important. Viking women wore their hair long. They left it flowing loose until they married, then tied it in an elaborate knot at the nape of their neck. Viking men also liked fancy hairstyles. They cut their hair short at the back, but let their fringes grow very long. So that they could see where they were going, some Vikings plaited the strands that hung down either side of their face.

▲ Fashionable Viking hairstyles. Women also wove garlands of flowers to wear in their hair on special occasions.

Skilled craftworkers

51 **Vikings made most of the things they needed.** Viking families had to make – and mend – almost everything they needed – from their houses and its furniture to farm carts, children's toys and clothes. They had no machines to help them, so most of this work was done slowly and carefully by hand.

52 **Blacksmiths travelled from farm to farm.** Many Viking men had a simple smithy at home, where they could make and mend tools. For specialized work, they relied on skilled blacksmiths, who travelled the countryside, or they made a long journey to a workshop in a town.

▶ Blacksmiths heated iron over open fires until it was soft enough to hammer into shape to make tools and weapons.

53 Bones could be beautiful.

Skilled craftworkers used deer antler to make fine combs. But these were too expensive for ordinary Vikings to buy. They carved bones left over from mealtimes into combs, beads and pins, as well as name tags and weaving tablets (used to make patterned braid).

54 Craftsmen carved cups from the cliff face.

Deposits of soft soapstone were found in many Viking lands. It looked good, but it was very heavy. To save taking lumps of it to their workshops, stoneworkers carved rough shapes of cups and bowls into cliffs at soapstone quarries, then took them home to finish neatly.

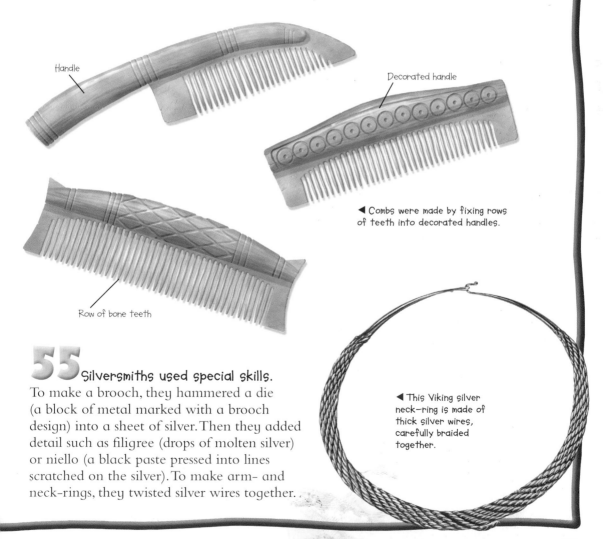

Handle

Decorated handle

◄ Combs were made by fixing rows of teeth into decorated handles.

Row of bone teeth

◄ This Viking silver neck-ring is made of thick silver wires, carefully braided together.

55 Silversmiths used special skills.

To make a brooch, they hammered a die (a block of metal marked with a brooch design) into a sheet of silver. Then they added detail such as filigree (drops of molten silver) or niello (a black paste pressed into lines scratched on the silver). To make arm- and neck-rings, they twisted silver wires together.

Viking towns

56 **Kings built towns to encourage trade.** Before the Vikings grew so powerful, merchants traded at fairs held just once or twice a year. Viking kings decided to build towns so that trade could continue all year round. Taxes were collected from the people and merchants who traded there.

▶ Viking markets were often held on beaches. Farming families and travelling merchants met there to buy and sell.

57 **Towns were tempting targets for attack.** Pirates and raiders from Russia and north Germany sailed across the Baltic Sea to snatch valuable goods from Viking towns. So kings paid for towns to be defended with high banks of earth and strong wooden walls. They also sent troops of warriors to guard them.

58 **Houses in towns were specially designed.** Space was limited inside town walls so houses were built close together. They were smaller than country homes, as people needed less space to store crops or house animals. Most town houses were made of wood with thatched roofs. Many had craft workshops and showrooms inside.

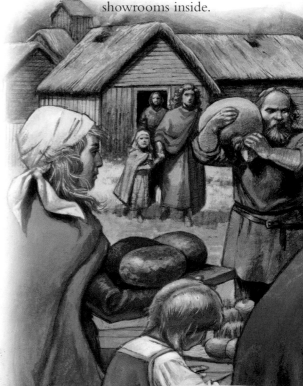

I DON'T BELIEVE IT!

The first Russians were Vikings! The name 'Russia' comes from the word, 'Rus', used by people living east of the Baltic Sea to describe Viking traders who settled there.

59 Towns made the first Viking coins.

As far as we know, there were no coins in Scandinavia before the Viking age. Traders bartered (swapped) goods, or paid for them using bits of silver, weighed out on tiny, portable scales. But many foreign coins came to Viking lands from overseas trading and raiding. Around AD825, craftsmen in the Viking town of Hedeby (now in north Germany) began to copy them. Later, other towns set up mints to make coins of their own.

60 Viking traders gave Russia its name.

Adventurous Vikings visiting the east shores of the Baltic set up towns as bases for trade. Some of the biggest were Staraja Ladoga and Novgorod, in Russia, and Kiev in the Ukraine.

◄ This Viking coin shows a merchant ship. It comes from the town of Hedeby.

Law and order

61 Vikings followed a strict code of honour. Men and women were proud and dignified and honour was important to them. It was a disgrace to be called a cheat or a coward, or to run away from a fight. Vikings also prized loyalty. They swore solemn promises to be faithful to lords and comrades and sealed bargains by shaking hands.

62 Many quarrels were settled by fighting. Quarrels between Viking families often led to feuds. If one family member was insulted or killed, all others had a duty to avenge him. Feuds could continue for months, with many people on both sides being killed, until each family was prepared to seek peace and pay compensation.

▲ Viking warriors challenged people who insulted them – or harmed their families – to a deadly duel.

63

Viking laws were not written down. Instead, they were memorized by a man known as the law-speaker. He recited them out loud every year so that everyone else could hear and understand them. Because of their expert knowledge, law-speakers often became advisors to kings and lords.

64

Every year, Vikings met at the Thing. This was an open-air assembly of all free men in a district. It met to punish criminals and make new laws. The most usual punishments were heavy fines. Thing meetings were great social occasions where people from remote communities had the chance to meet and exchange news. Many traders also attended, setting up stalls with goods around the edge a field.

▼ All free men – from noble chieftains to farmers – could speak and vote at a Viking Thing.

65

Ruthlessness was respected. It was tough being a Viking. Everyone had to work hard to survive and there was no room in the community for people who were weak, lazy or troublesome. Thieves were often hanged and criminals who refused to pay compensation or fines were outlawed. This was a very harsh penalty. Without a home and family, it was hard for any individual to survive.

QUIZ

1. What were the two worst Viking punishments for crimes? 2. How did the Vikings settle family feuds? 3. Why did Vikings shake hands with each other? 4. Who recited the Viking laws?

Answers:
1. Hanging and outlaw
2. By fighting – a duel
3. To seal bargains 4. The law-speaker

Games, music and sport

▲ Vikings loved magical, mysterious tales of dragons, elves and monsters – and exciting stories about famous local heroes.

66 **Vikings liked music, dancing and clowns.** At feasts, Vikings sang songs and danced. Depending on how much the guests had drunk, the dancing might be slow or riotous. Kings and lords also paid dancers, clowns, acrobats and jugglers to entertain their guests at feasts.

67 **Vikings laughed at jokes and riddles.** The Vikings had a rough, quick-witted sense of humour. They liked playing practical jokes and listening to stories about gods and heroes who defeated enemies by trickery. Vikings also played dice and board games such as chess and 'hneftafl' (king's table). But they were not good losers. Fighting often broke out at the end of a game.

▶ This board and counters were probably used for playing the game 'hneftafl', which was rather like chess.

68 Swimming, racing and jumping were favourite summer games. In summer, the weather was warm enough for Vikings to take off most of their clothes. This made it much easier for people to move freely and run and jump at greater speed. In winter, warmly-dressed Vikings liked snow-based sports such as cross-country skiing, as well as ice skating on frozen rivers and lakes.

▼ Viking archers used bows made of yew wood, strung with twisted plant fibres. Arrows were made of birch wood, with sharp tips made of iron.

I DON'T BELIEVE IT!

One favourite trickster story told how Viking god Thor – famous for his beard and huge muscles – dressed up as bride, with a veil, and pretended to marry a giant. Thor wanted to get back the magic hammer that the giant had stolen from him.

69 Viking sports were good training for war. Spear-throwing, sword-fighting and archery (shooting at targets with bows and arrows) were all popular Viking sports. They were also excellent training in battle skills and helped boys and young men to develop their body strength, get used to handling weapons and improve their aim.

70 Vikings liked watching wrestling – and fights between horses. Wrestling matches were also good training for war. A warrior who lost his weapons might have to fight for his life on the battlefield. But many Vikings watched wrestlers just for fun. They enjoyed the violence. They also liked to watch brutal fights between stallions (male horses), who attacked one another with hooves and teeth.

Gods and goddesses

71 **Viking people honoured many gods.**
The Aesir (sky gods) included Odin,
Thor and Tyr, who were gods
of war, and Loki, who was a
trickster. The Vanir (gods of
earth and water) included
Njord (god of the sea)
and Frey (the farmers'
god). He and his sister
Freyja brought
pleasure and fertility.

▼ Odin, Viking god of war, rode
an eight-legged horse. Two
ravens, Called Thought and
Memory, flew by his side.

▼ Beautiful Viking goddess Freyja rode
in a chariot pulled by cats.

72 **Animals – and people – were killed as
sacrifices.** The Vikings believed that they could win
favours from the gods by offering them gifts. Since
life was the most valuable gift, they gave the gods
living sacrifices. Vikings also cooked meals of meat
– called blood-offerings – to share with the gods.

73 **Destiny controlled the Vikings.**
According to legends, three sisters (Norns)
decided what would happen in the world.
They sat at the foot of Yggdrasil, the
great tree that supported the universe,
spinning 'the thread of destiny'. They
also visited each newborn baby to
decide its future. Once made, this decision
could not be changed.

74 After death, Vikings went to Hel's kingdom. Warriors who died in battle went to Valhalla or to Freyja's peaceful home. Unmarried girls also joined Freyja, and good men went to live with gods in the sky. Most Vikings who lived ordinary lives and died of illness or old age could only look forward to a future in Niflheim. This was a gloomy place, shrouded in freezing fog, ruled by a fierce goddess called Hel.

▶ Vikings asked fierce and furious god Tyr to help them win victories.

75 Towards the end of the Viking age, many people became Christians. Missionaries from England, Germany and France visited Viking lands from around AD725. The Vikings continued to worship their own gods for the next 300 years. Around AD1000, Viking kings, such as Harald Bluetooth and Olaf Tryggvason decided to follow the Christian faith as it helped strengthen their power. They built churches and encouraged people to be Christians.

▼ Njord was god of the sea. He married the giantess Skadi, who watched over snowy mountains.

QUIZ
1. Who was Loki?
2. What tree supported the universe?
3. Where did warriors go when they died?

Answers:
1. A trickster god
2. Yggdrasil 3. Valhalla

Heroes, legends and sagas

◄ Vikings loved sagas – stories that recorded past events and famous peoples' lives.

76 **Vikings honoured heroes who died in battle.** They told stories, called 'sagas', about their adventures so that their name and fame never died. These stories were passed on by word of mouth for many years. After the end of the Viking Age, they were written down.

77 **Skalds sang songs and told saga stories.** Viking kings and lords employed their own personal poets, called skalds. A skald's job was to sing songs and recite poems praising his employer, and to entertain guests at feasts. Most skalds played music on harps or lyres to accompany their poems and songs.

78 **Vikings feared that the world might end.** There were many Viking stories foretelling Ragnarok – the Doom of the Gods. This would be a terrible time, when the forces of good clashed with the powers of evil. Viking gods would fight against giants and monsters – and lose. Then the world would come to an end.

▼ Viking legends told how the world would come to an end at the battle of Ragnarok. They also promised that a new world would be born from the ruins of the old.

79 The Vikings believed in spirits and monsters. They were unseen powers who lived in the natural world. Some, such as elves, were kindly and helpful. They sent good harvests and beautiful children. Others, such as giants who ate humans, were wicked or cruel. Vikings often imagined monsters as looking like huge, fierce animals. They carved these monster heads on ships and stones to scare evil spirits away.

▲Vikings believed that Valkyries – wild warrior women – carried men who had died in battle to live with Odin in Valhalla (the hall of brave dead).

◀A Viking silver amulet (lucky charm), shaped like Thor's hammer.

QUIZ
1. What did Vikings call the end of the world?
2. Who did skalds praise?
3. Why did farmers wear hammers round their necks?
4. What did giants eat?

Answers:
1. Ragnarok 2. Their employer 3. To bring fertility to fields and animals 4. Humans

80 Lucky charms protected warriors and farmers. They wore amulets shaped like the god Thor's magic hammer as pendants around their necks. Warriors believed that these little hammers would give them extra strength in battle. Farmers hoped they would bring fertility to their fields and animals.

Death and burial

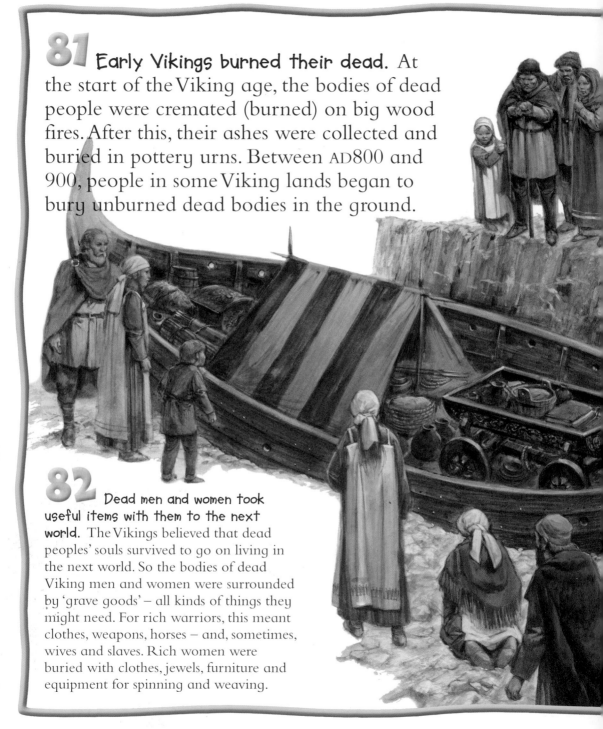

81 **Early Vikings burned their dead.** At the start of the Viking age, the bodies of dead people were cremated (burned) on big wood fires. After this, their ashes were collected and buried in pottery urns. Between AD800 and 900, people in some Viking lands began to bury unburned dead bodies in the ground.

82 **Dead men and women took useful items with them to the next world.** The Vikings believed that dead peoples' souls survived to go on living in the next world. So the bodies of dead Viking men and women were surrounded by 'grave goods' – all kinds of things they might need. For rich warriors, this meant clothes, weapons, horses – and, sometimes, wives and slaves. Rich women were buried with clothes, jewels, furniture and equipment for spinning and weaving.

83

Viking graves have survived for hundreds of years. Archaeologists have discovered many collections of grave contents, in remarkably good condition. Some, such as jewellery, pottery and stone carvings, are made of materials that do not rot. Some, such as clothing, have survived by chance. Others, such as ship burials, have been preserved underwater. All have provided valuable evidence about life in Viking times.

▼ These stones arranged in the shape of a ship's hull mark an ancient Viking burial ground.

◀ The dead were laid to rest in cloth-covered shelters on board real ships. Then the ships were set on fire so that their souls could 'sail away' to the next world.

84

Vikings hoped that ships might carry their souls away. So they surrounded buried cremation urns with ship-shaped enclosures of stones. Some enclosures were very large – up to 80 metres long – and were probably also used as places of worship. Very important Viking men and women were cremated or buried in real wooden ships, along with valuable grave-goods.

85

Vikings treated dead bodies with great respect. They washed them, dressed them and wrapped them in cloth or birch bark before burying them or cremating them. This was because the Vikings believed that dead people might come back to haunt them if they were not treated carefully.

I DON'T BELIEVE IT!

Some Viking skeletons and wooden ships that were buried in acid soils have been completely eaten away. But they have left 'shadows' in the ground, which archaeologists can use to find out more about them.

Writing and picture stories

86 **Many ordinary Vikings could not read or write.** They relied on the spoken word to communicate and on memory to preserve details of land, family histories and important events. At the beginning of the Viking age, all Vikings spoke the same language, the *donsk tunga* (Danish Tongue). But after AD1000, different dialects developed.

87 **Viking scribes wrote in 'runes'.** There were 16 letters, called runes, in the Viking alphabet. They were used for labelling valuable items with the owner's name, for recording accounts keeping calendars and for sending messages. Runes were written in straight lines only. This made them easier to carve on wood and stone. The Vikings did not have paper!

▲Viking runes. From top left, these symbols stand for the sounds: F U Th A R K H N I A S T B M L R.

▼ Vikings used sharp metal points to carve runes on useful or valuable items.

Deer antler with runes carved on it

Viking calendar

Comb with runes showing owner's name

88 **Runes were used to cast magic spells.** Sometimes, runes were used to write messages in secret code, or even magic spells. These supposedly gave the objects they were carved on special power. Some secret Viking writings in runes still have not been deciphered today.

▲ Rune stones were written records of Viking citizens.

89 Rune stones told stories. Wealthy families paid for expert rune masters to carve runic inscriptions on stones, praising and commemorating dead parents and children. Some boastful people also had stones carved with details of their own achievements. When the carvings were completed, the rune stones were raised up in public places where everyone could see them.

90 Picture stones told of great adventures. In some Viking lands, people carved memorial stones with pictures, instead of runes. These show scenes from the dead person's life and details of their adventures, together with pictures of gods, giants and monsters.

▲ Some picture stones told of people's achievements, others commemorated loved ones who had died.

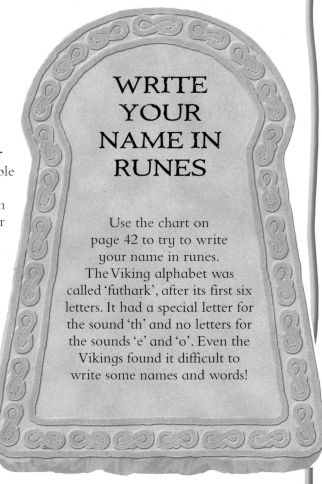

WRITE YOUR NAME IN RUNES

Use the chart on page 42 to try to write your name in runes. The Viking alphabet was called 'futhark', after its first six letters. It had a special letter for the sound 'th' and no letters for the sounds 'e' and 'o'. Even the Vikings found it difficult to write some names and words!

The end of the Vikings

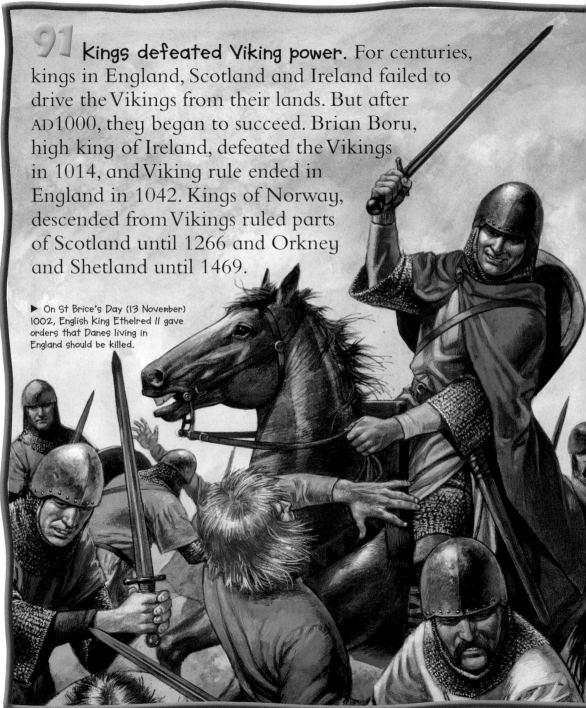

91 **Kings defeated Viking power.** For centuries, kings in England, Scotland and Ireland failed to drive the Vikings from their lands. But after AD1000, they began to succeed. Brian Boru, high king of Ireland, defeated the Vikings in 1014, and Viking rule ended in England in 1042. Kings of Norway, descended from Vikings ruled parts of Scotland until 1266 and Orkney and Shetland until 1469.

▶ On St Brice's Day (13 November) 1002, English King Ethelred II gave orders that Danes living in England should be killed.

92 Vikings learned to live alongside other peoples. In most places where Vikings settled, they married local women and worked with local people. Some of their words and customs blended with local ones, but many disappeared. Viking traditions only survived if the place where they settled was uninhabited, such as Iceland, or the Orkney Islands, off the north of Scotland.

▲ In 1066, the Normans — descendants of Vikings who had settled in Normandy, France — invaded and conquered England. This scene from the huge Bayeux Tapestry (embroidered wall-hanging) shows their Viking-style ships.

93 Christianity destroyed faith in Viking gods. The Vikings believed their gods, such as Thor and Odin, would punish them if they did not worship them, and would kill Christian missionaries. But the missionaries survived. So did Vikings who became Christians. This made other Vikings wonder if their gods had any powers, at all.

◄ Christians living in Scandinavia after the end of the Viking age made statues of Jesus Christ to stand in their churches, as symbols of their faith.

94 Vikings set up new kingdoms outside Viking lands. In places far away from the Viking homelands, such as Novgorod in Russia, or Normandy, in northern France, Viking warlords set up kingdoms that developed independently. Over they years, they lost touch with their Viking origins, and created new customs, laws and lifestyles of their own.

95 Viking settlers abandoned America. Soon after AD1000, Thorfinn Karlsefni, a Viking merchant from Iceland, led over 100 Viking men and women to settle at Vinland — the site in North America where Lief Eriksson landed. They stayed there for two years, but left because the Native North Americans attacked them and drove them away.

Viking survivals

96 **Some days of the week still have Viking names.** The Vikings honoured different gods on different days of the week. We still use some of these gods' names in our calendars. For example, Wednesday means 'Woden's Day', Thursday means 'Thor's Day' and Friday means 'Freya's Day'. In modern Scandinavian languages, Saturday is called 'bath-day', because that was when the Vikings had their weekly bath!

97 **We still use many Viking words today.** In countries where the Vikings settled, they spoke Viking languages and gave Viking names to their surroundings. Many Viking words for everyday things still survive such as 'sister', 'knife' and 'egg'. Many places in northern Europe still have Viking names, such as 'Thorpe' (outlying farm), Firth (river estuary), Cape Wrath (Cape Turning-point) or 'Kirkwall' (Church-bay).

98 **A Viking story inspired Shakespeare's most famous play.** William Shakespeare (1564-1616) lived over 500 years after the Vikings. He used one of their stories to provide the plot for one of his best-known plays. It tells the story of Hamlet, a prince in Denmark, who cannot make up his mind what to do after his father is murdered.

▶ In Shakespeare's play, the tragic hero Hamlet thinks deeply about the meaning of life – and death.

99 **People still celebrate Viking festivals.** For example, in the Shetland Isles, where many Vikings settled, people celebrate 'Up-Helly-Aa' on the last Tuesday in January. This marks the end of Yule, the Viking mid-winter festival. They dress up as Vikings, parade through the streets, then burn a lifesize model of a Viking warship.

100 **Father Christmas was originally a Viking god.** Yule (mid-winter) was one of the most important Viking festivals. Vikings held feasts then and exchanged presents. They also believed that Viking gods travelled across the sky, bringing good things – just like Father Christmas!

▶ Today, as in Viking times, the light and warmth of blazing fires at mid-winter festivals bring hope and cheerfulness at a cold, dark time.

▲ This modern picture of Father Christmas shows him riding through the sky in a Viking-style sleigh, pulled by reindeer from Viking lands.

Index